G000167992

A COMPETENCE PERSPECTIVE ON LIFELONG WORKPLACE LEARNING

PROFESSIONS - TRAINING, EDUCATION AND DEMOGRAPHICS

Additional books in this series can be found on Nova's website under the Series tab.

Additional E-books in this series can be found on Nova's website under the E-books tab.

A COMPETENCE PERSPECTIVE ON LIFELONG WORKPLACE LEARNING

CHRISTIAN STAMOV ROßNAGEL
STEFAN BARON
BRIGITTE M. KUDIELKA
AND
KLAUS SCHÖMANN

Novinka
Nova Science Publishers, Inc.
New York

LIBRARY OF CONGRESS CATALOGING-IN-PUBLICATION DATA
A competence perspective on lifelong workplace learning / Christian Stamov Rossnagel ... [et al.].
  p. cm.
  Includes index.
  ISBN 978-1-61668-686-4 (softcover)
  1. Organizational learning. 2. Employees--Training of. 3. Career development. 4. Adult learning. I. Rossnagel, Christian Stamov.
  HD58.82.C652 2010
  658.3'124--dc22
                    2010015565

Published by Nova Science Publishers, Inc. ✝ *New York*

CONTENTS

PREFACE

An ageing workforce and skilled labour shortage create the need for workplace learning well beyond middle adulthood. With only a minority of older workers participating in training and development programmes, participation rates of older employees clearly need to increase. In this book, we adopt a competence perspective that treats workplace learning as a trainable skill, rather than as a cognitive function. Consistent with this view, competence should be accessible to interventions from human resource development professionals. By the same token, successful workplace learning across the lifespan depends on appropriate incentive structures and work conditions that in turn require specific institutional support and a policy context that fosters lifelong learning. After the introduction, we give in the second chapter an overview of findings on cognitive ageing and what their implications for workplace learning competence are. Also, we summarise some of our recent research on age-related competence differences. In the third chapter, we suggest direct and indirect strategies to foster lifelong workplace learning. In the fourth chapter, we address the needs for institutional support and policy reform to enhance lifelong learning.

Chapter 1

INTRODUCTION

The ageing of the workforce and the pressures of globalisation create a need for workplace learning well beyond middle adulthood (Vaupel & Loichinger, 2006). Consequently, initiatives to promote lifelong learning are on many companies' agenda. It seems understood that older workers will have to participate in training and development who in the past have not been the target group (Ilmarinen, 2006). It seems much less understood whether older workers are equipped to meet such demands. Research has reliably established sizeable age-related cognitive decline (Baltes, Lindenberger, & Staudinger, 2006) and consistent with this, older workers are often perceived as resistant to change and slow in acquiring new material (Nelson, 2002). Indeed, Ng and Feldman (2008) in their meta-analysis found a weak, but negative correlation between age and training performance, confirming the meta-analytic finding from Kubeck et al. (1996) that older workers in comparison to their younger colleagues showed less mastery of training material and took longer to complete training programmes.

In this book, we adopt a competence perspective. In essence, this implies that workplace learning, rather than being a function of cognitive capabilities, is a trainable *skill*. Lifelong workplace learning will therefore be subject to secondary, rather than primary age effects. Whilst primary effects stem from age-related cognitive decline, secondary effects are rooted in motivational factors. As a consequence, they are more open to human resource development interventions than primary effects. By the same token, successful workplace learning across the lifespan depends on appropriate incentive structures and work conditions that in turn require specific institutional support and a policy context that fosters lifelong learning.

We address these issues in three chapters. In the subsequent chapter, we give an overview of findings on cognitive ageing and what their implications for workplace learning competence are. Also, we summarise some of our recent research on age-related competence differences in learning competence. In the third chapter, we suggest direct and indirect strategies to foster lifelong workplace learning. In the fourth chapter, we address the needs for institutional support and policy reforms.

Chapter 2

LIFELONG WORKPLACE LEARNING: FROM STEREOTYPES TO EVIDENCE

Even in today's workplace, there are wide-spread stereotypes about older workers. Employers value older workers' loyalty and experience, but are concerned about their flexibility, readiness to adjust to changing circumstances, and technological competencies. Hansson et al. (1997) noted that some 86 % of Fortune2000 companies stated they valued older employees, yet only 23 % of the same companies had policies that allowed for hiring older workers. As far as training is concerned, older workers are seen to learn slowly, possess insufficient computer skills, and show poor training performance (Simon, 1996). Younger workers consider their peers to be better qualified for their jobs and to have a greater potential for development than their older colleagues (Finkelstein, Burke, & Raju, 1995).

How much truth is there in these stereotypes? Does older workers' ability to learn actually decline as a result of cognitive ageing? We address these questions in the first part of the chapter by looking at key results from cognitive ageing research. In the second part of the chapter we describe learning competence as a key driver of learning motivation. Finally, we summarise some important organisational and individual sources of age-related competence changes.

2.1. COGNITIVE AGEING AND LEARNING ABILITY

The aforementioned stereotypes are partly rooted in the popular belief that most cognitive abilities show linear decline from as early as young adulthood (Schaie, 2005). This view seems to be justified in light of classic intelligence testing studies that arrived at similar findings. Terman (1916) for instance assessed the intelligence of children and young adults from a variety of age groups. Yerkes (1921) studied the intelligence profiles of more than one million US Army recruits. Jones and Conrad (1933) measured intelligence in almost 1,200 people between ages 10 and 60. Similar to Terman and Yerkes they posited their findings showed intellect growth to peak at between 18 and 21 years of age. This peak was followed by linear albeit slower decline as a result of which adults at age 55 regressed to the level of 14 year-old children. In sum, these and similar studies established the *Deficit Model of Ageing*, portraying age as a period of decline and decreasing abilities – a bundle of deficits in comparison to younger people. Tornstam (1992) referred to this as the *misery perspective* on ageing.

It was not until the Mid-1950s when it dawned upon researchers that the cross-sectional method had its flaws. Computing from the comparison of people from different age groups a growth curve involves quite a leap of generalisation. It does not take into account so called *cohort effects*, i.e. differences in intelligence as a result of different life experiences (e.g., differential schooling). As a consequence, researchers increasingly focussed on *longitudinal* studies. Research with participants who had been tested repeatedly starting from childhood revealed that several cognitive abilities remained stable well into middle or even older adulthood (e.g., Bayley & Oden, 1955).

Contemporary research draws a far more differentiated picture of age-related change in cognitive abilities. For one thing, researchers distinguish at least two sources of age-related changes: neuropathology and disuse. Also, studies take two levels of cognitive functioning into account: fluid and crystallised intelligence. Neuropathological ageing refers to changes in the nervous tissue of the brain that will occur even in healthy adults as an inevitable consequence of ageing (Gunning-Dixon & Raz, 2003). Disuse may lead to the same phenomena as neuropathological ageing (e.g., lower test scores), albeit for quite different reasons. A well-known variant of disuses in work contexts is *obsolescence*. It refers to skills becoming obsolete as a result of technological change (Charness & Schaie, 2003), requiring the acquisition of new skills. Some workers will tend to avoid the very tasks that require newly-learnt skills. Such workers might then be perceived to show age-related decline, which actually has nothing to do with neuropathological ageing.

As early as 1920, Foster and Taylor realised that there are two types of cognitive processes. Jones and Conrad (1933) concluded from their results that older people had an advantage on tests that allow for using previous experiences. Horn and Cattell (1996) coined the terms *fluid* and *crystallised* intelligence for these different processes. Fluid intelligence refers to those cognitive resources that people use for dealing with novel information and without relying on earlier learning. Crystallised intelligence, on the other hand, is used in tasks that refer to previous knowledge and experiences.

It has been shown in a number of longitudinal studies since the 1950s that fluid abilities do indeed decline across the life-span. In one of the most comprehensive studies, the *Seattle Longitudinal Study* (cf. Schaie, 2005), cohorts of 25 year-olds were tested every seven years, starting in 1956 and with new cohorts recruited at every wave. A broad range of cognitive abilities from verbal, spatial and numerical thinking to memory tasks to tests of processing speed was assessed. Schaie noted that measures of fluid intelligence such as processing speed and numerical thinking show decline from as early as 25 to 32 years of age, whilst verbal fluency and language comprehension increase until middle adulthood only to remain stable afterwards. On these two dimensions, there were no statistically significant differences between participants at 25 and 88 years of age.

Lindenberger and Baltes' (1994) report of the *Berlin Aging Study* fits with this picture and suggests that a decline in sensory function is the fundamental mechanism of cognitive ageing. Data from older adults between ages 70 and 103 years showed decline on virtually all cognitive tests (e.g., processing speed, reasoning, memory, general knowledge, verbal fluency). At the same time, decline in visual and auditory acuity accounted for the decline in the cognitive tests. Lindenberger and Baltes argued that sensory acuity reflected the brains general fitness, which in turn influences higher cognitive functions. Analysing the data from adults between 25 and 103 years of age, Baltes and Lindenberger (1997) showed cognitive decline to be independent of education, profession, social status or income. Cognitive decline thus appears to be a fundamental biological mechanism.

Whilst fluid intelligence declines invariably with age, crystallised intelligence remains stable or even shows slight gains well into older adulthood, i.e. way beyond current legal retirement ages. Crystallised intelligence is the basis of knowledge and experience. It comes into play when novel information is to be integrated into existing knowledge. Crystallised and fluid intelligence interact to shape intellectual development across the life-span (for a recent overview, cf. Baltes, Lindenberger, & Staudinger, 2006) and crystallised intelligence may serve to compensate for age-related decline in fluid intelligence. Throughout their development people appear to follow the principles of Selection, Optimisation, and Compensation: they select their strongest areas of intellectual functioning, optimise performance in these areas by training and practice, and compensate for age-related losses by using alternative strategies or abandoning once-pursued goals.

Salthouse (1984) conducted a classical study on the compensation of fluid decline. He investigated the mechanisms behind older secretaries' typewriting performance: although measures of general information processing indicated slower processing in older secretaries, their typewriting speed in copying text was at a par with their younger colleagues. It turned out that older typists were able to read longer passages of text parallel to typing, compensating for their slower reading speed. Apparently, their expertise in switching between reading and typing had allowed them to select the strategy of memorising longer passages instead of switching back and forth often. They optimised this strategy by extending their reading span and so compensated for the decline in reading speed.

Phillips, Kliegel, and Martin (2006) showed that such compensation applies also to more complex processes. They had younger and older participants "plan a day": The task was to get a number of things done (e.g., paying bills, visit a friend, do the shopping) within a certain time in a fictitious town. Participants got a map and a list with the shop opening hours and distances between shops. Like in Salthouse's study, older participants scored lower on fluid cognitive ability measures. However, they scored higher on information selection, i.e. they were better able than younger participants to focus on information relevant for carrying out the task and to ignore irrelevant information. In this manner, they compensated for losses in fluid resources.

What are the implications of cognitive ageing research for learning ability? Will older workers be able to compensate for fluid decline through crystallised intelligence? Actually, we posit that this would be the wrong question to ask for a number of reasons. Fluid abilities do go down but this does not mean that learning ability will go down, too.

Most importantly, cognitive decline has been demonstrated in a testing-the-limits approach; study participants carried out cognitively demanding tasks under time and instructional constraints. In many cases, performance decrements have been measured by comparing the time to task completion between older and younger participants. Older people may indeed take as much as three to four times longer on complex arithmetic operations, but we are looking at differences of a few seconds here and it has not yet been satisfactorily established what this means for real-world learning operations. In workplace learning, people more often than not are in control of the process. They may arrange the context according to their needs, most of all, there will not be the time constraints imposed on laboratory participants. Related to this, fluid decline appears to be quite pronounced above age 70. Decline will be measurable long before that age, but it may be questioned whether it will play a large role in everyday work (cf. Park, 2000).

Secondly, laboratory research focuses on investigating "pure" processes and in fact "contamination" of fluid processes from crystallised processing is avoided by using abstract tasks. As the Phillips et al. example above has shown, ageing effects may disappear as soon as compensation is no longer disallowed. Again, real-world workplace learning will in most cases not be a "process-pure" task. As people may choose learning strategies that support linking novel information to their existing knowledge, they can support compensation processes.

In sum, we think it is safe to conclude that cognitive ageing will not so much impinge on cognitive learning *ability*, but on motivational learning *readiness*. Older workers are in a quite different situation than their younger colleagues. Their general view on work changes and they benefit less from theory-oriented teaching. Younger colleagues may readily absorb conceptual content that they can be sure to apply at some later point in their career. With older workers' shorter time horizon, acquiring knowledge that is ready to use in the Here and Now becomes more important.

2.2. THE ROLE OF LEARNING COMPETENCE

We summarise under workplace learning any intentional learning that serves to acquire or extend work-related knowledge and skills (cf. Matthews, 1999). Workplace learning may come as formal, non-formal, or informal learning. Formal and non-formal learning take place in traditional off-the-job classroom settings, with the certification of formal learning being the only difference between the two types. Both formats are mainly instructor-led. Informal learning, in contrast, is organised by learners themselves in the first place and more often than not happens in the workplace.

Informal learning borders on work-integrated learning and can take the formats of instructions from supervisors or colleagues, using computer-based trainings for self-study, mentoring programmes, job rotation, or quality circles. In recent years, there has been a shift from formal and non-formal *training* to informal *learning* (cf. Streumer, 2004; Cross, 2007). Clarke (2004) considers informal learning to be one of the most important recent trends in the workplace that partly arose from the concern that off-the-job learning may often be far from the realities of the workplace. It may therefore impair the transfer of knowledge to the job and may lack relevance to workers' needs. Informal learning, in turn, is seen to promote the acquisition of experience-based knowledge, which is tailored to the work context. It is based on real-life problem-solving and situated within a specific social context.

The fact that informal learning is mainly learner-led implies that it requires a high degree of self-regulation. This means that learners must be able to self-diagnose their learning needs, set specific goals, choose appropriate strategies to attain these goals, and evaluate their learning in terms of progress towards goals. Consistent with our competence perspective, we assume that learning ability alone does not warrant successful learning; learning *competence* needs to supplement ability. Learning competence is of particular importance given the aforementioned shift from training to informal learning. Informal learning requires learners to identify their learning needs, to develop from this their learning goals, to select appropriate strategies, and to monitor and evaluate progress towards goals. Efficient strategy use and the investment of mental and time resources will depend on learning orientation and epistemic beliefs. We summarise these three levels of competencies under the term of learning competence. This competence is *not* an ability or talent, but "a roughly specialised system of abilities, proficiencies, or individual dispositions to learn something successfully" (Weinert, 1999, S. 44). Unlike intelligence, learning competence can itself be acquired and improved by training.

Learning competence comprises the three levels of cognition, meta-cognition, and motivation. On the cognitive level, people memorise the content and make it accessible for subsequent application. They may use a variety of strategies to best reach their learning goals; these strategies include repetition, elaboration, and organisation strategies (Weinstein & Mayer, 1986). Repetition strategies focus on surface features of new information, for example the pronunciation of words in a foreign language or terminology. They serve the purpose of consolidating this surface information in memory. Elaboration strategies support the integration of novel information into existing knowledge. Important strategies include cognitive structuring, constructing examples, brain storming, and cognitive mapping. Organisation strategies aim at structuring new knowledge and focus on the links between units of knowledge. Two classical organisation strategies are summarising text and using schemata. Text summaries get learners to work out the conceptual relationships in text information and thus promote deep-level understanding. Schemata are a set of problem-solving and information processing strategies that can be routinely applied to novel information, for example, asking guiding questions when searching for and compiling information on a novel topic.

Meta-cognitive strategies work one level above cognitive strategies. Whilst the former may be seen as the learning proper, meta-cognitive strategies structure and control that learning. People use meta-cognitive strategies to identify their knowledge and skill gaps, set their learning goals based on that information, and monitor their progress. Also, they use them to choose appropriate learning strategies.

The motivational level of competence comprises more than the simple willingness (or unwillingness!) to learn. People have relatively stable learning *orientations* that may be captured as *intrinsic* or *extrinsic* learning motivation. Intrinsically motivated people learn for the fun of broadening their horizon, acquiring new skills, and deepening their knowledge. Extrinsically motivated people use learning to reach goals beyond the learning, for example, to move into a higher position. With regards to ageing, negative aspects of extrinsic motivation become relevant; workers may focus on avoiding failure and concealing lack of skills and knowledge, which may trigger inefficient learning behaviours or even learning avoidance. Closely related to motivational orientations are *epistemic beliefs*. They are subjective assumptions on what knowledge is and how learning should proceed. It is obvious that learners who take for granted that knowledge is an objective reality that is "handed down" by authorities will learn differently than learners who regard learning as active problem solving and knowledge construction. Maurer et al. (2003) have shown that older workers tend to hold lower beliefs in the malleability of skills through training than their younger colleagues; this belief is likely to strongly influence learning motivation.

The cognitive and meta-cognitive strategies that make up learning competence may be applied to basically any type of content; they are general learning tools. This raises the question for what types of workplace learning they will be relevant. Is learning competence only for the informally learning worker where demands for self-regulation are high? It seems obvious that only those will learn successfully who will be able to reliably identify their learning needs, to use efficient learning strategies, and to evaluate their learning in a goal-oriented manner.

Nevertheless, high levels of learning competence will be useful even in traditional instructor-led courses where the need for self-regulation is a lot lower. In formalised learning, goals are usually set and learning methods are selected as guiding questions for text study, role play, or focus groups are used. However, learners will still need to monitor their learning. They can hardly rely on the instructor to determine if they are learning and have learnt what they need for their job. Learners must see for themselves if they manage to integrate into their knowledge the contents that are presented. In this respect, learning competence is important also in instructor-led formal and non-formal trainings and seminars, even if to a lesser degree.

What does successful learning mean? Workers do not usually get assessed for their learning performance. What they have learnt will have to stand the test of work; to the extent that they manage to use their newly learnt knowledge and skills, they may be seen to have succeeded.

There is more to successful learning, however, than just being able to apply new knowledge and skills. Workplace learning places various psychic demands on learners. On top of the cognitive effort of learning proper, learners must invest time and effort in keeping up motivation and concentration, deal with negative affect. Moreover, learning is just *one* of their tasks in the workplace; it adds to their workload and may thus cause learning stress. In this view, successful learning means to learn in accordance with one's personal resources and to minimise the strain from learning. Paulsson, Ivergård, and Hunt (2005) showed that learners who were able to control their learning process found competence development more stimulating and experience less learning-related stress. As learning competence helps workers optimise control of their learning, it may be seen as a good way of preventing the negative effects of learning-induced workplace strain. According to the Job-Demand-Job-Control model introduced by Karasek and Theorell (1990), strain at the work place predominantly results from high (quantitatively and qualitatively) job demands combined with low job control in terms of individual skill discretion and decision latitude. To date, convincing evidence has shown that exposure to an adverse psychosocial work environment in terms of high demands and low control elicits sustained stress reactions resulting in job strain and negative long-term health consequences (Siegrist & Marmot, 2004) as well as reduced workplace performance (Kwakman, 2001). On the other hand, this intriguing model explicates in the so-called "active learning"-hypothesis that a work environment characterised by high job demands combined with high job control in contrast promotes the development of high learning activity, learning motivation as well as the development of further skills (Karasek & Theorell, 1990). In accordance with the Job-Demand-Job-Control model, Paulsson, Ivergård, and Hunt (2005) concluded that if a learner has a high level of control (or participation) of her/his process of learning, the learning outcome improves. Likewise, Taris et al. (2003) found that job control had a positive effect on learning, although the highest levels of learning and self-efficacy were observed when control was high and demands low. To conclude, in order to optimally support lifelong learning at the work place, high job control combined with a reasonable amount of job demands should be a key feature of a good working environment.

In respect to strain and learning at the work place, one should also be aware of the fact that acute as well as chronic stress can potentially impact on learning and memory processes via the release of stress hormones caused by a physiological stress reaction (Lindau, Almkvist, & Mohammed, 2007). Within recent years, substantial knowledge has accumulated in this area and has led to a much better understanding of the specific effects of stress and acute stress hormone secretion on human learning processes (Joels et al., 2006; Lupien & Maheu, 2007; Wolf, 2007). For example, until now it is known that the stress hormone cortisol, which is released via the hypothalamus-pituitary-adrenal (HPA) axis, enhances memory consolidation but impairs delayed retrieval of previously learned material. Furthermore, acute stress which is unrelated to a task impairs performance. It is of note, though, that the effects of acute stress are additionally modulated by gender, age, as well as the emotional valence of respective learning material. Concerning long lasting strain, chronic stress is mostly associated with impairing effects on memory and the integrity of memory-related brain regions like the hippocampus (Wolf, 2003). To conclude, in order to prevent substantial negative effects of stress and stress-related hormone secretion on learning processes at the work place, chronically stressful work conditions should be avoided to maintain an advantageous working environment.

2.3. First Evidence on Age Differences in Learning Competence

We have outlined above the widespread beliefs that age will inevitably be associated with declines in learning performance (cf. Nelson, 2002). Such stereotyping might impinge on workers' training motivation (cf. Maurer, 2001) and lead to older workers doubting their learning abilities and the malleability of their skills (e.g. Maurer et al., 2003). Data are now needed, as informal workplace learning has often been treated in conceptual pieces (cf. Streumer, 2004, or with methodologies other than those building on a self-regulation framework. Our own research (Schulz & Stamov Roßnagel, in press; Stamov Roßnagel et al., 2009) suggests both that the view on informal learning as a form of self-regulated learning is justified and that informal learning competence might change across the lifespan more as a function of contextual influences, rather than of normative factors related to "inevitable" cognitive decline. In an exploration of age-related differences in informal learning competence (Schulz & Stamov Roßnagel, in press), we had 479 workers between 18 and 65 years old from a German mail-order company rate their learning strategies and metacognitive learning control in informal learning episodes. Participants also completed ratings on their training and development participation within two years prior to the survey, their learning success (e.g., keeping with their schedule, ability to transfer learnings to the workplace, learning problems), their learning motivation in terms of *learning approach motivation* (desire to extend one's knowledge and skills) and *learning avoidance motivation* (desire to conceal one's deficits in skills and knowledge), the company's general learning and training climate (Tracey & Tews, 2005), learning opportunities at work, and their memory self-efficacy, i.e., the judgement of one's memory ability (Zelinski & Gilewski, 2004).

Results showed that the learning competence dimensions of learning control (i.e., ability to set learning goals and monitor one's learning progress) and learning approach motivation predicted learning success, whilst there was no relationship between age and learning success. The relationship between learning control and learning success was mediated by memory self-efficacy (MSE). High-MSE participants used more control strategies, which positively affected learning success. Thus, learning competence as expressed in learning control and learning approach motivation ratings and learning success did not directly depend on age, but on participants' judgements of their memory abilities. There were more low-MSE participants in the older workers (51 years and older) group; these participants reported lower learning success despite a positive learning orientation and a sufficient learning strategies repertoire. Of the learning context variables, learning opportunities showed a stronger relationship with learning success than training and learning climate. Irrespective of age, workers with higher learning competence, i.e. better learning control and higher levels of learning approach motivation, reported more frequent training and development (T&D) participation. Participants with lower learning competence indicated greater difficulty in planning their T&D activities and a stronger need for learning support.

We objectified these self-report findings in an experimental study (Stamov Roßnagel et al., 2009) in which we were particularly interested in the role of memory self-efficacy, which we had identified as a mediator of learning success. Low-MSE might affect the *cognitive resource allocation* during learning, i.e. the effort learners invest. Previous research (e.g., Stine-Morrow et al., 2006) showed that younger low-MSE learners invest more effort (i.e., study time) to difficult items than to easier items, whilst the opposite applies to older learners. As this effect so far has only been shown for rather elementary learning tasks (reading of short text passages), we assessed whether similar effects would be found for the rather complex learning in work-related contexts. In an e-learning environment, 60 participants (30 each in the younger – 18-35 years old – and older – 51-65 years old – groups) worked on a learning unit on team building. In addition, we assessed learning competence with the measures from the above-described learning competence analysis, computer learning experience as a control variable, and working memory span as a measure of memory capacity. This served to separate the roles of "genuine" age effects from age-related cognitive decline and "motivational" age effects from decreased memory self-efficacy.

We found lower learning performance for older participants; at the same time, the influence of memory self-efficacy differed as a function of age both for learning performance and for study time. Younger and older participants with high-MSE invested the same amount of study time, whilst older low-MSE learners used less study time than their younger counterparts. Similarly, whilst MSE did not affect the learning performance of younger participants, older low-MSE participants attained lower performance than their high-MSE peers. Regression analysis showed that the learning competence variables predicted learning performance ($R^2 = .24$, $p < .01$, $\beta = .36$).

These results are of course preliminary in that the learning success ratings from the survey cannot directly be compared to the learning performance data from the experiment. Still, these findings might help raise a couple of useful research questions. For instance, in the questionnaire, participants referred their ratings to a variety of learning formats including non-computer-based, highly self-regulated formats. Such learning likely provides opportunities for compensating age-related cognitive decline and might lead to higher perceived learning success and eventually learning performance. An interesting question for future research would thus be whether different degrees of "self-regulatability" (SRL) are associated with different magnitudes of age effects.

Another issue concerns the malleability of SRL competence. The findings on the role of memory self-efficacy suggest that given their belief of having rather poor memory capacity, older participants invested less learning effort, which decreased learning performance. Such memory beliefs might substantially be influenced by the learning opportunities companies offer. Our ongoing research with other companies suggests that the relationship between older workers' T&D participation and memory self-efficacy is moderated by the companies' learning and training climate. In sum, it appears that analysing learning competence from an SRL point of view might be useful and helps predicting informal learning performance.

Chapter 3

PROMOTING INFORMAL
LEARNING COMPETENCE

We have shown in the previous section that older workers' learning ability will normally remain intact across their entire work life. To turn this ability into learning success, workers will need a specific learning competence. It is not a "stand-alone" competence but is influenced and constrained by a variety of individual and organisational dimensions. An effective strategy of enhancing learning competence will have to take into account these dimensions as part of strategic, "demography-proof" personnel management. There is no single tool, let alone one that fits all companies. Only an integrated strategy will have a lasting positive effect on workers' learning competence and help make life-long learning a reality. In the first part of this section, we deal with the prerequisites for *indirect* and *direct* competence promotion strategies, which we address in the second and third part, respectively, of this section.

3.1. ANALYSING THE LEARNING
SITUATION AND PLANNING
INTERVENTIONS

Age-differentiated training and development depend on their being tailored to climate and diversity management, which in turn influence a company's *learning situation*. Organisational variables such as the age and training climate set the stage for learning competence to unfold and any strategy to enhance competence will address these constraints if they are to yield lasting effects. In essence, promoting older workers' learning requires a) an analysis of the company's learning situation, b) intervention planning based on this analysis, and c) implementation in line with the principles of dynamic personnel management.

The learning situation of a company is determined by three components: age and learning climate, learning competence profiles, and learning resources. These components are closely interdependent: a company with a positive learning climate is likely to provide adequate learning resources, which will in turn positively affect learning competence. Still, the three components may have been developed to different degrees, and it will thus be important to assess them independently.

Assessing Age and Learning Climate

The influence of learning and training climate has been extensively studied in recent years and various questionnaires are available for climate assessment. Age climate is a relatively new construct (cf. Noack & Staudinger, 2007), but can be reliably assessed with questionnaire measures similar to learning climate measures. The climate assessment should include both workers and management. Comparing climate indices reported by these two groups will help reveal dissatisfaction potentials and areas of improvement.

Assessing Learning Resources

Information on learning resources may be collected from personnel management and supervisors. *Social* and *material* resources alike should be assessed. Beyond a company's offers of formal and non-formal training, material resources include databases, job-related company libraries, and computer-based trainings. Quality circles and worker forums would count as both material and social resources. Internal and company-endorsed external mentors and instructors are amongst the most important social learning resources.

Assessing Learning Competence

The three levels of competence (learning strategies, control strategies, and self-regulation) as described in section 2 are at the heart of learning competence analysis. Unlike learning resources, competencies will be assessed with workers. Building on earlier self-regulated learning questionnaires, we have in co-operation with large companies from various industries compiled a competence assessment tool that may be administered on-line in less than 15 minutes. Beyond the core competencies, analysis should include support needs for learning and learning difficulties. Competence assessment results may be compared to supervisors' information on learning resources. This will help identify learning barriers and room for improvement of learning support.

As learning situation analysis includes both learning competence proper and its organisational boundary conditions, it allows for three strategies of competence enhancement: direct and indirect promotion, and a combined strategy. During intervention planning, competence gaps should thus be analysed in relation to these boundary conditions to determine what strategy will be most beneficial. For instance, some workers might possess a rich learning strategies repertoire and positive learning orientation, but may not be able to apply their learning strategies to complex learning episodes, reflecting a lack of control strategies. Other workers might show a high learning competence level, but report a lack of learning resources. In this case, indirect promotion (i.e., adequate learning resources) would be helpful. In the former case, direct promotion would be the intervention of choice, including a control strategies training during a learning-to-learn workshop.

Learning competence analysis might reveal the existence of learner groups with problematic learning orientation. First results from our demographic network show that some workers might exhibit increased learning anxiety coupled with low competence beliefs. In this case, successful learning would be impaired even in the presence of sufficient learning and control strategies. Also, some workers might be resistant to learning due to low beliefs in the efficacy of training and to a perceived lack of social support and recognition of learning efforts. With such learners, simple strategy trainings would yield little to no effect. Training should rather address the motivational component of learning competence.

3.2. INDIRECT PROMOTION

Indirect promotion of learning competence consists of designing a learning environment that requires and supports the use of learning competence. Rather than being an alternative to direct promotion, indirect promotion is linked in several ways and complements direct promotion. Firstly, the effects of direct promotion will depend on indirect promotion to the extent that a restrictive learning environment may prevent successful use of learning competence, thereby weakening the effects of competence trainings, which are a form of direct promotion. Secondly, environments supporting informal learning require at least some learning competence and direct promotion may provide this basis. Thirdly, training research has shown that the effects of strategy trainings alone are limited, but can be increased by providing a learning-conducive environment.

3.2.1. Climate Management

Organisational climate research has extensively described a variety of facets of climate and investigated effects on job satisfaction, job-related well-being or innovation behaviours. Much less is known about active climate management. Climate cannot be changed with a simple tool and by "order from above", but some ground rules are available to avoid an unfavourable climate.

Transparent Information Should Replace Implicit Myths
We have shown how outdated myths on older workers' learning ability may threaten learning motivation. It is obvious that replacing these myths by evidence-based information on the difference model of ageing will be a key to establishing a positive age and learning climate. Gossip and stereotypes will run counter to any climate management efforts. Spreading adequate information will require *transparent* communication. Stereotypes tend to become beliefs and it will be important to acknowledge the existence of these beliefs if they are to be overcome. Transparent communication also means to include *all* workers and not just a "chosen few" multipliers who might be perceived as "passing on information from above". For instance, one of our demographic network partners holds regular video conferences with all workers. Top-level managers, including the CEO, communicate important

developments and trends. Workers are free to submit questions beforehand, which are answered during the conference. Measures like these are good steps on the way to open and transparent communication.

Age Differentiation ≠ Age Discrimination

Older workers may feel stigmatised by companies offering different trainings for different age groups and the good intentions of age differentiation may turn into age discrimination. This does not mean of course, that any age differentiation should be given up only to avoid discrimination. If companies keep offering age-neutral training that takes only middle-aged workers' learning needs into account, they will merely produce latent discrimination rather than avoid discrimination altogether.

The first step to avoiding this situation is the aforementioned analysis of the company's learning situation. Assessing the climate perceptions and learning needs of different age groups provides important information on how to tailor the internal communications strategy. Communications should focus on describing age-related changes in individual learning behaviour and should emphasise that different behaviours may still lead to the same learning success. Moreover, it should be stressed that age-differentiated training helps maintain learning competence across work life, enabling workers to more flexibly adapt to changing requirements, thus providing them with more control of their own work.

Learning Climate

In a positive learning climate, workers share the firm belief that any learning – even if it incurs mistakes – is useful for workers and the company alike and that it promotes individual and company growth and development. In today's circumstances of pressure to succeed and limited budgets such "romantic ideals" may be less than easy to achieve. Still, a few suggestions might help to avoid unnecessarily negative climate.

For instance, differential encouragement for training is a thing to avoid even if it is based on the supposedly good intention of "sparing older workers the hassle of learning". Inviting younger workers to participate in training whilst ignoring their older colleagues may have a double negative effect. Firstly, older workers may feel to be perceived as unable or unwilling to learn. Moreover, this would signal to workers that the company is the sole beneficiary of the training and that individual development plays no important role. If this were not the case, older workers would have to be encouraged just like their younger colleagues. In line with this, it is also a good idea to not exclusively offer directly work-related training but to include, for example, soft skills courses in order to signal that the company is interested in and supports workers' individual development.

Direct communication between workers and supervisors may be the most powerful means of establishing a positive learning climate. Professional communication is characterised by explicit feedback that is behaviour-oriented rather that focusing on personal traits: concrete examples of good performance and of ways of improving performance should be given wherever possible. Mistakes and errors should be seen as learnings on the way to improved performance and negative sanctions should be avoided. Also, it is very important to invite workers' own view on potentials for improvement and support needs, and discuss with them what they can do themselves to work in line with their needs and abilities. Finally, letting workers participate in work design wherever possible increases the chances workers diagnose their own learning needs and applications of their knowledge.

In order to enable supervisors and managers to communicate professionally, special training may be necessary. Lack of knowledge of age-related changes in learning competencies and learning needs may incur a variety of difficulties in supervisor – worker communication. "Benevolent helplessness" may make younger supervisors give only superficial and hardly informative feedback to older workers in an attempt to avoid discrimination and maintain a positive climate. An adverse variant may be inappropriate comparisons of older and younger workers that may leave older workers with a feeling of being defeated in the competition with the young.

3.2.2. Creating a Learning-Conducive Environment

Work design research provides valuable insights how work environments and tasks may be arranged in a way that enables and encourages workplace learning (cf. Morgeson & Campion, 2003). Skill Variety, Task Identification, and Job Control from Autonomy and Feedback are influential drivers of work motivation and it turns out that these characteristics are also important for supporting workplace learning (cf. Richter, 2005).

Job Control
Job Control refers to all aspects of workplaces and tasks that enable workers to exert some sort of influence on their own work. Control includes perceived *cognitive control* that pertains to workers' perception of overseeing

the context of their own job within their department or even the entire company. Feeling "linked to the whole" increases task identification and thus influences learning motivation. Typical dimensions of job control are decisions on the speed and sequence in which work tasks are carried out, or on task planning itself. Also, performance feedback is a dimension of job control. Finally, workers perceive higher levels of job control if they feel informed about trends and facts in their company, and if they are allowed to participate in developing work tasks.

Time Resources

Workplace learning takes time for a variety of reasons. Firstly, learning may proceed alongside normal work, no matter whether learning comes as dialogical instruction from colleagues, as use of media or as work-integrated problem solving. Secondly, new knowledge may need to be documented and transferred to colleagues and team members. Finally, extra time can support workers' systematic trying of new work procedures that may be the basis for improved and innovative solutions. Innovative workers appear to use extra time for knowledge creation from experimenting and dialogical instruction.

Learning Resources

On top of material resources (databases, computer-based trainings, etc.), social resources are an important ingredient of learning-conducive environments. Mentors or tutors can promote *double loop learning* (Argyris & Schön, 1974) that goes beyond optimising pathways to set goals, but that leads to defining new goals. Double loop learning rests on connecting distributed knowledge in networks of experts from different specialties. Such networks may reach beyond normal workgroups and often beyond departments.

Personal Development

Workers need goals for their personal development. Such goals should reach beyond traditional vertical careers as longer work lives and higher proportions of older workers make such goals increasingly unattainable. Horizontal careers provide plenty of opportunities but to date seem to be undervalued. In a learning-conducive environment, horizontal career options are laid out and portrayed as worthwhile paths of development that are of high value to both company and workers. Job rotation across departments, supported by specialised training, may be used to train cross-departmental experts. Company and individual goals should overlap as much as possible to support learning motivation, if the company is the only beneficiary of development, motivation might be minimal.

Task-Specific Training

Many shop-floor workers receive minimal feedback on their work. Thus they hardly have any insight into improving the quality or efficiency of their work. In a similar way, a lack of quality standards in service professions may make feedback from clients difficult to interpret. In sum, working with minimal feedback may lead to adverse routinisation effects, skill obsolescence and learning competence decline. Regular training on task simulations and critical incidents analyses may prevent such effects, keep skills up to date and increase workers' awareness of room for improvement. Task-specific training can compensate for a lack of learning opportunities and address the particular learning needs of work groups.

3.3. DIRECT PROMOTION

Indirect promotion of workplace learning encourages workers to use their learning competence, but may at best improve this competence. Indirect promotion cannot, however, replace systematic competence training nor is it a remedy to competence deficits. Workers must possess at least basic competence to benefit from the material and social resources provided through indirect promotion. If learning competence assessment reveals systematic competence deficits, particular learning or support needs, or even certain problematic learning styles, indirect promotion should be supplemented by direct promotion that comes in the form of strategies and self-regulation workshops.

Learning and control strategies and self-regulation can by definition be improved through training. Any such training should only be implemented after a comprehensive and differentiated learning competence analysis (cf. Section 3.1) that allows for a reliable diagnosis of competence deficits. Based on this diagnosis, effective trainings can be developed with an appropriate combination of strategies and self-regulation exercises. Learning and control strategies may easily be taught in an isolated fashion for use as "learning tools", yet, trainings that address learning strategies alone will be an exception rather than the rule. Research has shown that the success of strategy trainings will largely depend on these trainings addressing learning competence in a holistic fashion. It has long been known that practising learning strategies in a stand-alone manner will yield only short-lived effects that will hardly transfer to novel learning episodes (cf. Paris & Jacobs, 1984; Palincsar & Brown, 1984). Including metacognitive strategies and self-regulation into trainings should thus be the preferred option.

Hofer and Yu (2003) included in their training a general unit on the processes of learning before practising the very learning strategies. In a similar way, learning competence workshops should include a general session that introduces the competence concept and the interplay of the three competence levels. Workshop participants may then apply the cognitive and metacognitive strategies presented during the workshop to cases from their everyday work. They may for instance construct problem-solving schemata, practise techniques of structured information gathering from textbooks, and train the organisation of new knowledge by means of visualisation methods (tables, graphs, mind maps, etc.). Independent of the effects of using learning strategies, the knowledge of the interdependency of learning and control strategies or the development of learning barriers from negative learning orientations will yield insights into successful learning and create a basis for flexibly transferring learning and control strategies to different learning episodes.

Learning diaries are an important ingredient of competence workshops and it should be ensured they are used wherever possible. Workshop participants note in their diaries any experience that is relevant for their learning outside the workshop. For instance, they may record any question or doubt that stirred their thinking about opportunities and limitations of the learning and control strategies they used. These questions may then be used for case work in the next workshop. Landmann (2005) used semi-structured diaries, in which participants noted their questions. In addition, they completed standardised questionnaire scales immediately before and right after their learning episodes. Scales referred to self-set goals, chosen strategies, and learning-related affect and motivation. Landmann found that this format increases self-reflection and enhanced the use of learning and control strategies.

Chapter 4

IMPROVING THE INSTITUTIONAL SUPPORT AND POLICY CONTEXT FOR LIFELONG LEARNING

Programmes to promote lifelong learning, like a mechanical toolbox, come in all shapes and sizes, and with country-specific features. In the sphere of learning, all programmes are inextricably linked to their context, particularly when looking at differences in a public or private institutional setting. Besides general declarations of the need for lifelong learning for all, realistic accounts of potential policy support focuses on well defined target groups and reforms of the institutional framework to facilitate access to lifelong learning. We will thus consider them in turn: the broader policy context of lifelong learning, the institutional framework and the tools.

Lifelong learning is unquestionably the pivotal factor for enterprise success, especially in times of demographic change and a rising shortage of skilled employees. Despite its importance, the CVTS III (Continuing Vocational Training Survey) data for Germany indicate that a large number of enterprises (30 %) did not offer continuous vocational training in 2005. More than two-thirds of enterprises provide continuous vocational training and 54 % of all enterprises offer the "classical" form of training in the sense of seminars or courses. Enterprise size strongly affects the provision of training. Only 44 % of all enterprises with 10 to 19 employees provide formal training, while 95 % of all enterprises with at least 1.000 employees do so (compare figure 1).

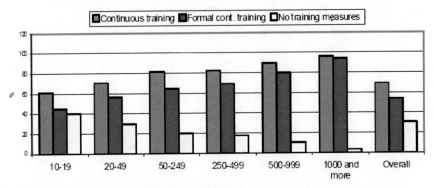

Source: Federal Statistical Office, CVTS III 2007.

Figure 1. Continuous training offers (by enterprise size). - Enterprises with ... employees -.

The sector of activity of an enterprise still predetermines training opportunities of its employees. Nearly all enterprises in the financial services offer continuous training, only half of the enterprises in the building industry, the catering and hotel business provide any form of continuous training (see figure 2).

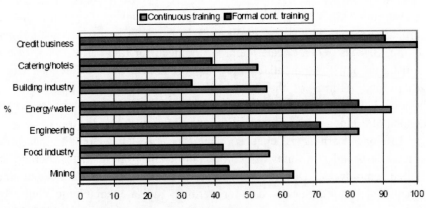

Source: Federal Statistical Office, CVTS III 2007.

Figure 2. Continuous training offers. (selected branches).

The IAB-Establishment Panel 2003 contains additional data for the reasons of non-participation in continuous training of firms. Forty-Five percent of firms, which did not offer any continuous training, cited already having sufficient qualification as justification for their behaviour, while nearly 14 %

of the firms cited a lack of adequate financial resources to train their employees. Around 13 % of the firms don't offer any continuous training in general.

4.1. THE POLICY CONTEXT

Lifelong learning is not a stand-alone system. Learning is an integral part of the workings of both the economy and society, and since it cannot be considered apart from them, each country's lifelong learning system is as unique and individual as the country itself. However, just as there are patterns in production and welfare organisation across states, lifelong learning systems of many countries share similar features. Different systems of economic, social and welfare organisation promote distinct types of learning outcomes, policy and practice. Countries apparently choose two distinct routes to providing protection to citizens against labour market and social risk. One would be to provide social security, and the other – to focus on education. In terms of security, some states focus on universal rights to social insurance that aim to strengthen the position of the individual against market forces, and make sure that everyone can have a suitable living standard without having to rely on the market. This type of states is called social-democratic welfare states (e.g., Sweden and Denmark). Others, called continental or conservative welfare states (Germany, France, Austria), focus on securing individuals in the job market through work-life insurance and strong job protection. A third type, called liberal welfare state (US, UK, Ireland), have limited the role of the state to a minimum and rely predominantly on market forces and low levels of social insurance.

In terms of educational and lifelong learning outcomes, liberal states take educational opportunity as an alternative to the policies of social democratic states, and the work-related insurance prevalent in continental states. Since liberal states are in general concerned with promoting flexibility and social mobility, they not only dedicate the highest share of expenditure to education, but would also tend to promote general education tracks which pave the way for better occupational mobility. Continental welfare states, which target the preservation of the social status quo rather than social mobility are expected to have high expenditure, and will tend to sort people into specific, or vocational, education tracks. Finally, social democratic states will spend a relatively lower share of total expenditure on education, but nonetheless a larger absolute amount due to their generally higher social expenditure (Hega & Hokenmaier, 2002; Iversen & Soskice, 2001).

What does this distinction mean in terms of adult learning outcomes? The labour market structure and arrangements prevalent in liberal welfare states is expected to encourage adult education, since this is one of the few ways to achieve a degree of insurance against large life course unemployment risks. Due to the structure of careers characterised by a large degree of occupational mobility, we can expect that adult training will also be more general. In continental states, adult training will tend to be more vocationally oriented, with the aim of securing the position of the individual within the firm or sector of the economy. Social democratic states also boost high participation levels since their lifelong learning programmes are better financed, more comprehensive in scope, and resting on the strong support structure of the social security system (which provides better public financing and more opportunities to engage in training).

Understanding how the training systems vary across states is key to understanding why some tools work in certain contexts and some do not. For example, in the context of strong job protection in a country, an employee will invest little in general skills, but once unemployment occurs, the lack of general skills becomes a very significant problem leading to longer unemployment. The key point here is that in designing solutions to promoting lifelong learning, policy makers need to pay attention to the context, how the policy relates to the labour market conditions, firm's employment practices and macro-economic preconditions.

Public training programmes need to be coherent and to achieve this, they cannot be constrained to the field of training alone. To illustrate, consider the case of a programme for training of unemployed single mothers. Even if training is free, the beneficiary will need to know of the opportunity (i.e., information and guidance systems need to be in place), be able to support herself (that is, unemployment benefits will need to provide a training allowance), and have access to the time necessary to enrol in the course (i.e., free or subsidised childcare needs to be available). Even in this simplified case, should only one of the conditions be missing, the programme is likely to fail.

Large-scale reforms work only if combined with corresponding reforms in social security and labour market policy that provide a coherent policy approach. For example, delaying actual average retirement age for years rather than months gives a real push to the further training of "silver workers". Institutional path dependency is important to consider when designing policy and understanding its context. Previous policies both produce the need for change, and hinder change at the same time. For example, many industrialised countries used to focus on promoting low-wage and low-skilled work in conjunction with specialisation in production in order to reduce unemployment. While it did work at the time, this policy has now resulted in a large number of people both urgently needing qualifications and skills, while being very reluctant to learn and having very few opportunities to do so.

4.2. THE INSTITUTIONAL FRAMEWORK

The institutional framework in the field of lifelong learning is the support structure on which training policy is based, in its design, delivery, monitoring and evaluation. The number of actors involved in the process of designing and implementing policy is typically very large, with lifelong learning in most cases being subject to the influence of one or two Ministries (the Ministry of Education and the Ministry of Labour and Social Policy), numerous government agencies (qualification authorities, regional and local inspectorates, guidance services, quality control), the Public Employment Service (for the unemployed), various sectoral, regional or local employer or employee associations, training providers, NGOs, the enterprise, and seemingly last – individuals. While all actors have the goal to encourage lifelong learning, they have very different ideas on what this learning should be, what purpose it should serve, and who the beneficiaries should be. Organising and channelling these divergent interests to make the most out of available resources is the task of the institutional framework. Denmark, known for its creative combination of flexibility and security for employees has pursued a successful integration of the many actors in the field of training.

Innovative learning cultures focus on continuous training throughout the life course. This is the result of profound changes in the way the economy works and the way that the labour market is pushed to provide more performance and high-quality human resources than ever before. With knowledge becoming the cornerstone of economic development, past systems of training have been with no exception overwhelmed, and even new systems are still finding it hard to keep in pace. Therefore, designing a public institutional framework to underpin this new learning culture is a significant challenge. While it is hard to pinpoint one model that works best, there are some general guidelines that any project to reform the institutional system in the sphere of lifelong learning should follow.

Ensure Smooth Coordination between National Institutions

A close interaction between education, training, labour market, and social policy is absolutely necessary to make headway (OECD, 2003). To this end, a coherent policy framework should exist pinpointing exactly the responsibilities and powers of each institutional actor and setting standard procedures under which dialogue for policy creation can take place. Dialogue always needs to be the first step of policy design, in order to ensure that the framework remains coherent, and that policies complement rather than compete. Thus, formalised contacts between institutions (such as obligations for consultation, joint advisory bodies, etc.), as well as informal networks between people (via, e.g., regular joint meetings, workshops and forums) allowing for the quick diffusion of information and knowledge among policy makers, are both essential.

Make Sure Institutions Are Transparent

This principle can be paraphrased as "less is more" in terms of institutional structure. The fewer institutions there are, and the more clearly defined their responsibilities, the easier it becomes for persons seeking tailor-made training courses to obtain adequate qualifications effectively (Mytzek & Schömann, 2004). Transparency in the overall training market and its institutions is the key and the equivalent to accessibility and understanding. For example, recent reforms in Ireland have placed qualifications in the mandate of a single national institution, and have relocated many award-making powers from a number of diverse institutions to only two agencies (OECD, 2007). Even so, however, institutions need to be diverse enough to be able to meet the wide variety of individual needs.

Make Sure Institutions Are Open

Learning being an activity embedded in diverse contexts (community, social, and the workplace), it is clear that institutions cannot be closed systems with little or no external feedback. To ensure this, policy needs to respond meaningfully to the requirements of the community, the workplace and the individual. This responsiveness can be achieved only through involving all relevant agencies together with employers, trade unions, as well as regional and local communities in the process of (local) policy development and implementation. This can help build local ownership of programme results, can improve the relevance of programmes to needs and can help clarify these needs in the first place. A number of countries have established such mechanisms for involvement, including stakeholder advisory forums or advisory bodies comprising stakeholder representatives and other instruments for consultation regarding policy, joint scenario building working groups comprising stakeholder representatives aiming to forecast and manage the development of training systems, or have given the social partners voice and managerial involvement in the development of training policy and practice (e.g., the dual system in Germany or the national qualifications framework in the UK).

4.3. THE TOOLS

The tools available to policy makers in the field of lifelong learning are about as numerous and varied as the contexts in which they were created. However, they are all embedded, by virtue of their design and use, in the overall lifelong learning policy. This policy framework defines them and assigns their functions, much like the field of engineering assigns direction and meaning to simple tools such as a hammer or a screwdriver. Lifelong learning policy is a distinctive field, with its defining features. Compared to mainstream educational policy, it is characterised by four key features (OECD, 2004):

A Systemic View

As opposed to the sectoral approach of education policy, lifelong learning policy covers the whole range of possible forms, avenues and motivations for training. As such, it takes an integrated view over both supply and demand of training, across all sectors and regions in a state.

Centrality of the Learner

Lifelong learning policy is learner-oriented and not supply-oriented. That is, it does not only cover institutional arrangements for provision of skills, but places the focus on meeting individual needs through a wide spectrum of approaches.

Motivation (and Ability) to Learn

Unlike formal education, lifelong learning policy needs to put much more focus on building individual capacity to acquire new knowledge and skills. Since lifelong learning is often informal, distributed across time and taking place in different contexts, policy needs to build the basic skills required for an individual to participate (also known as "learning to learn") and the motivation, focus and discipline required to complete a qualification or acquire a skill *while* working.

Multiple Objectives of Learning Policy

In recognition of the fact that lifelong learning may take different forms and directions according to the motivation of the individual (career development, personal growth, pursuing social, cultural or civic goals), policy needs to be very well aware of how these motivations differ along target group, and even within individuals over time.

In this context, specific programmes work on several levels, each corresponding to a (more or less) distinct section of the decision making process involved in making a commitment to train.

4.3.1. Motivation

Motivation is the first key precondition to participation in learning. As we have detailed above, in order to complete and profit from the learning process, people need to be strongly motivated to succeed. A first step, then, is to persuade people that training is something they need for their personal and professional growth. There are three main approaches to this problem: making beneficiaries aware of training needs, making benefits of training larger, and/or making them clearer. All of these instruments are crucial in promoting participation.

First, the target group needs to be made aware of the fact that they lack certain skills, and that gaining these skills will bring about some benefits.

There are examples of nationwide campaigns to promote knowledge and skill acquisition, such as Ireland's national literacy initiative, or the Adult Learners' Week in the UK. For the UK initiative, publicity includes a large number of local events; press articles, TV coverage, and telephone help lines. Such campaigns and events have the capacity to stimulate interest as a first step. However, most initiatives run on the local level and have an active outreach component for involving the disadvantaged, who are likely to have high barriers to training and whose belief that they do not need training will therefore be untroubled by general passive information campaigns. The example of learning ambassadors practiced in the Netherlands and the UK is a case in point. In the Netherlands, the city of Tilburg engaged formerly illiterate people to promote its literacy program through informal contacts, personal relationships and face-to-face contact with beneficiaries.

In active outreach policies, it is not only the person who acts as a motivator that is important, but also the venue. In Korea, the Anyang Citizens Adult Education Centre delivers literacy courses and approaches women (one of its target groups) in places like bus stops, supermarkets and beauty shops. Similarly, in Denmark, guidance desks have been set up in busy places where they can be highly visible.

In order to ensure that training brings about higher and clearer benefits, qualification systems need to be made progressive so as to enable people to easily fit each new skill in the overall structure of their learning life. Even if the system is in place, however, qualifications can serve as currency on the labour market only as long as they are accepted as valuable by employers. The acceptance of qualifications is a long process which takes place gradually on the national level as qualification-related performance is observed, evaluated and acknowledged. Similarly, learners will put stock in qualifications only when these carry some value on the market (OECD, 2007). This process is time consuming and is highly dependent on the quality assurance mechanism in place.

A second distinct, but nonetheless related avenue for increasing returns to training is to ensure that the training is relevant to the needs of learners and enterprises. The responsiveness of the training system to evolving economic and labour market needs is a key focus of initiatives aimed at modernising education and training systems. Here again qualification systems play a significant role through serving as an institutional mechanism linking the education and lifelong learning system to the labour market. The focus in many countries has therefore been on enabling a smooth transition between theoretical knowledge and practical application. A best practice example is the transfer coaching in a company. The acquired knowledge in a training course is specifically adapted to the workplace of an employee through this transfer coaching.

Employers can step in to aid the definition of key competences, and the validation and recognition of competences earned throughout working life. Such a system would recognise and appropriately treat the workplace as a legitimate site of learning which can build the same competences as other sites within the education system. It would also make sure that programmes are relevant to the needs of the market.

4.3.2. Transforming Motivation into Action

Motivation to learn is unfortunately not enough to guarantee participation. In a second step, once interest is engaged, people need to be able to find a suitable type of training. By suitable, we mean available, cost-effective and responding to their needs. Within the lifelong learning framework, this function is carried out by information and guidance systems (IGS). Career guidance refers to services and activities intended to assist individuals, of any age and at any point throughout their lives, to make educational training and occupational choices and to manage their careers (OECD, 2004b, p.10). These IGS first aid individuals in finding out what type of qualification they need to gain the most in terms of their overall career development. Thus, at its best, information and guidance provides the beneficiary with a clear plan for career development, and goes forward to define the crucial skills that the beneficiary needs to acquire in order to put this plan into operation.

In Austria, Germany, the UK and the Netherlands among others, these services tend to have three levels: 1) web-based tools for self service, 2) relatively brief personal interviews and guidance often over the telephone, and 3) intensive guidance covering in-depth interviews and skills assessments, career planning, and training for the management of career and personal development. In this way, both efficiency of use of public funds, and effectiveness in appropriately serving all target groups, are ensured. The UK is a case in point, where a key reform is the integration of the learndirect national learning advice service with local Information, Advice and Guidance services. Adults who are low-skilled and/or from a social or economic priority area have access to personalised advice to help them overcome their barriers to learning. There is a strong focus on those who need the most help and who are least able to pay for it.

The enterprise is a key venue for provision of guidance and information for the employed, and a number of successful initiatives have demonstrated its capacity. In Austria, large firms provide guidance on learning opportunities through education and culture representatives on works councils. In Germany and the Netherlands, employability agreements are arrangements for periodical competence assessment and training, which are defined as reciprocal obligations for firms and workers. In the UK, the Employer Training Pilots have a very significant guidance component for (low-skilled) workers and (small and medium-sized) enterprises.

Evidently, however, there is still a long way to go towards fully capitalising on the potential of the work place to serve as an effective and successful venue for guidance. Successful practices towards that end include the introduction of incentives to stimulate career guidance in enterprises and the promotion of partnerships with relevant institutions to deliver workplace guidance (OECD 2004b). Additionally it needs to be ensured, that government-sponsored employee training programmes have a clear guidance component.

4.3.3. Ensuring Accessibility

Having successfully engaged the interest of beneficiaries, motivated them, and having guided them to the course that will serve their needs, the next step is to make sure that this course is accessible. There are several dimensions to access: time, financial, qualifications (institutional), comprehension- or skill-related, and physical. That is, beneficiaries need the time to engage in a course, the financial resources to participate, the qualifications that enable access to the course of study, the basic skills necessary to understand the course and make advantage of it, and finally they need a provider close, flexible, and good enough to deliver it.

The Time Dimension of Access
As training is integrated in the working and social life of individuals, it necessarily overlaps with other important activities, for example work or care. It is therefore crucial that the system for lifelong learning enables individuals to make the transition between these spheres. Social partners are beginning to take up this in their negotiations and collective bargaining. Two types of instruments are frequently applied. We discuss first career breaks and training leave. In Austria, employees who have worked with a firm for more than three

years are entitled to a career break of up to twelve months for educational purposes. The break has to be approved by the employer. It is financed by the state in the form of a monthly grant, and entitles employees to return to their previous position upon completion. Training leaves have two main features: they provide some sort of subsistence for the period of leave and they provide employees with the right to re-enter the firm on the same position as before upon completion (OECD, 2005).

The second element is flexible time arrangements. For less intensive courses where full-time study is not required, flexible time arrangements represent a good way of enabling access (OECD, 2005). Additionally, "timesaving", under which employees can save up extra hours of work and holidays in a time savings account, to be used whenever the individual needs some "separate time" for learning. The Netherlands have also designed a policy response to tackle issues of flexibility and combination of activities, through the Adjustment of Working Hours Act introduced in 2000. Under its provisions, all employees can put in a request to change working hours either upward or downward at any point, and employees need to honour their request except when precluded from doing so by conflicting business needs (Baaijens & Schippers, 2005). Job rotation schemes (where an employee on career break for training purposes is substituted by an unemployed person subsidised by the state) are another successful policy to enable access to sufficient time to engage in learning.

The Financial Dimension of Access

Since training carries significant benefits to individuals, employers, and the state, there is a strong argument that all three parties should share the costs as well. However, sometimes private actors are insufficiently motivated to provide the financing, or alternatively do not have the means to pay for training. Therefore, the state has an important role to play in both encouraging training overall, and promoting equality of opportunity for disadvantaged groups. Programmes enabling access to financial resources can be broadly grouped in two categories, depending on direct beneficiaries – individuals, or firms. For firms, traditional training promotion programmes are almost always centred on lowering the cost of training, and differ along the way they are financed. For example, a common instrument is the treatment of training as expenditure for tax purposes (i.e., firms are allowed to deduct training costs from their profits before taxes). This instrument is clearly investment-based, and while it does promote training, it does not enforce it. The second type of financing comes from training levies (nationally-or sectorally-imposed), the funds from which are then disbursed to eligible firms willing to train their workers. These instruments aim to reduce the incentive for "poaching" trained workers and motivate firms to train in a more direct way through penalising non-training firms. Such schemes exist in, for example, Belgium, Italy, Spain and Hungary on the national level, and the Netherlands, the United States, Denmark, and France on the sectoral level. Finally, the government may decide to directly finance training from general budgets, with such funds operating on the level of the European Union (the European Social Fund), the US, Mexico and Poland. Disbursement conditions have to be devised in a way to promote participation by smaller firms and disadvantaged groups. For individuals there is a wide variety of instruments available. Basic types are:

Income Tax Deductions: expenditure on adult learning is deducted from taxable income (in Austria, Denmark, Germany, Hungary, the Netherlands, and the US among others). This method is less effective however for low-skilled individuals who often pay little tax or none at all.

Individual Learning Accounts: these are tax-exempt savings accounts which can only be used for training purposes. They are financed on a "matching" basis, by individuals, firms, sectoral associations, and the government and represent perhaps the best available cost-sharing instrument. Additionally, they aim to promote individual ownership of the learning process, by both requiring an individual contribution to the account, and allowing people to make the choice on course subject and providers. However, these schemes are still relatively young and most countries have only attempted them on a pilot basis (the Netherlands, the UK, and the US). The UK scheme was shut down due to issues of fraud and the general failure of administrative procedures to ensure that training acquired met individual needs and quality standards. The Netherlands is also experimenting with a scheme of tax-sheltered individual savings accounts to finance unpaid leave.

Vouchers and Training Allowances: these two instruments are both based on government contributions with the aim of eliminating financial costs to learning. The difference between them is that vouchers (in Austria, Germany, Italy, etc) are used to cover direct costs of training (such as fees, study materials, etc.), and allowances (in Austria, Denmark, the Netherlands, the UK, Germany, etc.) cover indirect costs (such as foregone wages, subsistence, travel, etc.). Targeting of these can be achieved relatively simply by modulating access by priority groups (e.g., the low-skilled in Austria and Germany, or young and low-skilled adults in the UK).

The Qualification Dimension of Access

Sometimes access to further education and professional training is dependent on previous qualifications. Therefore, the entire system of qualifications should be set up in a way that promotes rather than hinders the lifelong acquisition of competences. Such life course-oriented qualification systems rely on the following major instruments (OECD, 2004b):

- Facilitating the transfer from non-accredited to recognised learning
- Accounting for, validating, and certifying informal and non-formal learning (also known as recognition of prior learning)
- Enabling credit transfer between learning tracks
- Designing qualifications in a way that facilitates the natural progression among qualification levels
- Making clear relationships between different qualification types; an instrument here is setting up national qualification frameworks (e.g., in Ireland and the UK)

Given that formal qualifications are hard to gain while in employment, since they require intensive effort over a long period of time, the process of recognition of prior learning (RPL) is a crucial access instrument. Recognising all learning and knowledge gained throughout the working life can aid to significantly shorten the time required to gain a qualification and thus lower both time and financial barriers to learning. Additionally, it can enable individuals with low or no qualifications to access learning previously closed off to them (e.g., university, specialised school, etc.). Current practice in the field is varied; however, in recognition of its virtue as an effective instrument, many countries implement some form of RPL. The process of recognising a competence also varies across states; however it always involves some sort of (practical) examination.

Some states, for example Denmark, Finland, the UK, the US, Sweden, etc., allow the recognition of skills and competences regardless of where these have been acquired and with no proof of course attendance. Others enable the partial recognition of knowledge with the aim to gain access to and get credit towards higher education degrees (incl. Austria, Norway, Spain, Sweden, etc.; OECD, 2005).

As is the case with any form of qualification, for RPL to work it needs to be accepted by the labour market. It is important to engage employers and educational institutions in the process and provide them with concrete evidence that RPL-based degrees are not second-rate to formal degrees, and that both signal the same quality of competence. This is why some states, for example the Netherlands and Portugal, have based RPL additionally on agreements with the social partners (OECD, 2005).

As much as RPL is an activation mechanism for the low-skilled, the very process of competence assessment may prove a barrier to some people, particularly those who have had previous unfavourable experience with formal education. Therefore, it is highly beneficial for the system to have assessment mechanisms and procedures adapted to the needs of disadvantaged groups. In qualification systems where the approach is to qualification attainment is outcome-based (or qualification-based, e.g., in the UK), this is less of a problem since learners have a good idea of what is expected of them and are less concerned about the evaluation process.

The Skill Dimension of Access

As states have been slow to move away from the job-for-life model emphasising one-off education at the beginning of the career to the employability-for-life model focusing on lifelong learning, some individuals lack the basic skills to engage in continuous training. *Basic skills*, or *key competences*, are a term which is often used in conjunction with long-term unemployment and social exclusion, and are defined as the skills necessary for an individual to fully participate in working life. These skills form the basis for lifelong learning as such, including the ability to follow and understand a course, and then translate its insights into everyday working life. Therefore, basic skills programmes are active in a number of states, such as the UK, with the aim to provide key competences to the entire population of a country to serve as the foundation for lifelong learning.

The curricula and approaches are varied; however they follow one single general framework. By definition, key competences are *transferable* (applicable in many contexts and situations) and *multifunctional* (can be used to achieve varying goals, solve different problems, and fulfil a variety of tasks). In the definition, elaboration and implementation of basic skills programmes, there is the need for a broad shift away from an emphasis on knowledge acquisition towards the *development of skills and attitudes* (Schömann & Siarov, 2005, Neugart & Schömann, 2002). There are several broad areas which key skills cover:

- **Communication in the Mother Tongue,** or the ability to clearly understand, communicate and express ideas in the mother tongue, in all contexts and situations

- **Communication in Foreign Languages** – understanding, communicating and expressing oneself effectively
- **Mathematical Literacy** in its simplest knowledge definition covers the understanding of numbers and basic operations: addition, multiplication, percentage and ratio calculations, etc. However, it also encompasses logical models of thought and analysis of the world, as well as analytical skills, abstraction and generalisation, critical thinking, building and applying models, etc.
- **Science and Technology** – using and manipulating technological tools and scientific approaches to solve everyday problems
- **ICT Skills**, which covers the ability to work with ICT tools (e.g., basic computer skills), as well as the skills to orient oneself and process large volumes of information, communicate and exchange information via these tools, etc.
- **Learning to Learn**, which covers skills related to the use and processing of information and its conversion into knowledge, the ability to translate theoretical knowledge into practical application, the ability to manage the learning process
- **Interpersonal, Intercultural and Social Competences**, or the ability to liaise with others, resolve social conflicts, interact with others, work in teams, and civic competences (the ones that allow the individual to participate in civic life), etc.
- **Entrepreneurship**, or the ability to both drive and accept change, to identify opportunities for personal, professional and social development, the ability to develop strategies and transform them into action plans for the achievement of a given goal, risk taking and risk assessment, etc.

Key skills also cover a number of values, which need to be accepted and internalised by individuals for their successful integration into and development of social, professional and civic life. These include understanding *the value of learning*, innovation, civic values, social tolerance and acceptance, entrepreneurship, self assessment and criticism, valuing and working with others, etc. Curricula should therefore be designed with this factor in mind in order to bring about a tangible change in individuals. The promotion of these values should be combined with targeted consultancy for minorities and genders, thus forming the second dimension of the key skills curriculum.

The Physical Dimension of Access

Ensuring that an effective delivery system exists is vital for the success of policies (Schömann & Leschke, 2004). On the regional level, the development of a large and diverse network of training providers is necessary in order to be able to meet learner needs. While diversity and the free growth of the system should be encouraged, this should go hand in hand with the development of a strong quality assurance system. Poor-quality programmes can be just as strong deterrent of participation as lack of financing, but have a longer-lasting effect. That is, once an individual has had a bad (especially first) experience with the lifelong learning system, this may irrevocably damage his/her trust in the system. Therefore, quality control and programme, provider and course monitoring and evaluation are key parts of the adult learning system. Governments play a crucial role via setting up legislation which promotes quality, making the quality assurance system and criteria clear to users, and disseminating information on providers conforming to quality regulations (OECD, 2005).

Beside the regional proliferation of training opportunities, an approach becoming increasingly more popular across states is to encourage the development of modular, part-time and distance learning programmes. For example, Germany has a network of evening schools that lead to vocational degrees free of charge, and in Austria secondary academic and vocational schools are open for adults in the evening. Weekend courses are also popular. The modularity of programmes enables individuals to easily fit the programme in their own schedule and progress with learning at their own pace (OECD, 2005), an approach embraced particularly by the UK and Switzerland.

Distance learning is also becoming more widespread, targeted mostly for either the very low-skilled, or the very high-skilled. The Open University in the UK is one of the oldest institutions of this type, and while some of its programmes do not require Internet access to follow, the general trend is towards more reliance on electronic means in the sphere. However, since distance learning participants have particular difficulties due to the fact that it requires strong motivation and good self discipline over a prolonged period of time, organising regular classes or advisee meetings with teachers is a good practice.

Chapter 5

CONCLUSION

With an ageing workforce on the one hand and the pressures of technological change and globalisation on the other hand, participation in further training needs to be increased in all age groups including older workers beyond 50 years of age. Contrary to popular belief and wide-spread age stereotypes, older workers' learning ability does not substantially decline, making successful participation possible at any age. What does decline, however, is learning readiness. We have shown numerous ways to increase learning readiness as a condition for increased training participation. With a focus on the individual worker, specific trainings are available to enhance older workers' learning competence, which many years after a worker's initial training often has undergone decline due to infrequent training opportunities. As far as the company level is concerned, the key to promoting lifelong learning lies in an age-positive working environment with tailored training offers and better accessibility, which might bring workers back to learning. This will require addressing supervisors' age stereotypes to help spread the knowledge that older workers by no means are inflexible and incapable of participating in training; more often than not all they need is regular training to maintain training and learning competence across the entire work life. Finally, on the policy level, institutional factors and policy context can provide the framework conditions for strengthening lifelong learning. These factors might include new and flexible arrangements like regional training co-operations.

REFERENCES

Argyris, C., & Schön, D. A. (1974). Theory in Practice – Increasing Professional Effectiveness. New York: Maxwell Macmillan International Publishing Group.

Baaijens, C., & Schippers, J. (2005). The Unfulfilled Preference for Working Fewer Hours in the Netherlands. *TLM.NET Conference Paper,* Budapest.

Baltes, P. B., & Lindenberger, U. (1997). Emergence of a powerful connection between sensory and cognitive functions across the adult life-span: A new window at the study of cognitive aging? *Psychology and Aging,* 12, 12-21.

Baltes, P. B., Lindenberger, U., & Staudinger, U. M. (2006). Lifespan theory in developmental psychology. In R. M. Lerner (Ed.), *Handbook of Child Psychology* (6th ed., Vol. 1, pp. 569-664). New York: Wiley.

Bayley, N., & Oden, M. H. (1955). The maintenance of intellectual ability in gifted adults. *Journal* of Gerontology, 10, 91-107.

Charness, N., & Schaie, K. W. (2003). *Impact of Technology on the Aging Individual.* New York: Springer.

Clarke, N. (2004). HRD and the challenges of assessing learning in the workplace. *International Journal of Training and Development,* 8, 140-156.

Cross, J. (2007). Informal Learning: Rediscovering the Natural Pathways that Inspire Innovation and Performance. San Francisco: Wiley.

Finkelstein, L. M., Burke, M. J., & Raju, N. S. (1995). Age discrimination in simulated employment contexts. An integrative analysis. *Journal of Applied Psychology,* 80, 652-663.

Gunning-Dixon, F. M., & Raz, N. (2003). Neuroanatomical correlates of selected executive functions in middle-aged and older adults: A prospective MRI study. *Neuropsychologia*, 41, 1929-1941.

Hansson, R. O., DeKoekkoek, P. D., Neece, W. M., & Patterson, D. W. (1997). Successful aging at work: Annual review 1992-1996: The older worker and transitions to retirement. *Journal of Vocational Behavior,* 51, 202-233.

Hega, G., & Hokenmaier, K. (2002). The welfare state and education: A comparison of social and educational policy in advanced industrial societies. *German Policy Studies,* 2, 1-29.

Hofer, B., & Yu, L. S. (2003). Teaching self-regulated learning through a "Learning to Learn" course. *Teaching of Psychology,* 30, 30-33.

Horn, J. L., & Cattell, R. B. (1966). Refinement and test of the theory of fluid and crystallized general intelligence. *Journal of Educational Psychology,* 57, 253-270.

Ilmarinen, J. (2006). Towards a longer worklife! - Ageing and the quality of worklife in the European Union. Helsinki: Finnish Institute of Occupational Health, Ministry of Social Affairs and Health.

Iversen, T., & Soskice, D. (2001). An asset theory of social policy preferences. *American Political Science Review,* 95, 875-893.

Joels, M., Pu, Z., Wiegert, O., Oitzl, M. S., & Krugers, H. J. (2006). Learning under stress: how does it work? *Trends in Cognitive Science,* 10, 152-158.

Jones, H. E., & Conrad, H. S. (1933). The growth and decline of intelligence: A study of a homogeneous group between the ages of ten and sixty. *Genetic Psychology Monographs*, 13, 223-298

Karasek, R. A., Theorell, T. (1990). Healthy work: stress, productivity, and the reconstruction of working life. New York: Basic Books.

Kubeck, J. E., Delp, N. D., Haslett, T. K., & McDaniel, M. A. (1996). Does job-related training performance decline with age? *Psychology and Aging,* 11, 92-107.

Kwakman, K. (2001). Work stress and work-based learning in secondary education: testing the Karasek model. *Human Resource Development International,* 4, 487-501.

Landmann, M. (2005). Selbstregulation, Selbstwirksamkeit und berufliche Zielerreichung. Entwicklung, Durchführung und Evaluation eines Trainingsprogramms mit Tagebuch zur Unterstützung des Self-Monitoring. Aachen: Shaker.

Lindau, M., Almkvist, O., & Mohammed, A. H. (2007). Effects of stress on learning and memory. In G. Fink, (Ed.), Encyclopedia of stress (2nd revised ed., Vol. 2, pp. 571-577). Oxford: Academic Press.

Lindenberger, U., & Baltes, P. B. (1994). Sensory functioning and intelligence in old age: A strong connection. *Psychology and Aging,* 9, 339-355.

Lupien, S. J., & Maheu, F. S. (2007). Memory and stress. In G. Fink (Ed.), Encyclopedia of stress (2nd revised ed., Vol. 2, pp. 693-699). Oxford: Academic Press.

Matthews, P. (1999). Workplace learning: Developing an holistic model. *The Learning Organization, 6*, 18-29.

Maurer, T. (2001). Career-relevant learning and development, worker age, and beliefs about self-efficacy for development. *Journal of Management, 27*, 123-140.

Maurer, T., Wrenn, K., Pierce, H., Tross, S., & Collins, W. (2003). Beliefs about "improvability" of career-relevant skills: Relevance to job/task analysis, competence modeling and learning orientation. *Journal of Organizational Behavior, 24*, 107-131.

Mytzek, R., & Schömann K. (2004). Transparenz von Bildungsabschlüssen in Europa. Sektorale Studien zur Mobilität von Arbeitskräften. Berlin: Edition Sigma.

Morgeson, F. P., & Campion, M. A. (2003). Work design. In W. C. Borman, D. R. Ilgen, & R. J. Klimoski (Eds.), *Handbook of Psychology* (Vol. 12, Industrial and Organizational Psychology, pp. 423-524). New York: Wiley.

Nelson, T. D. (2002). Ageism: Stereotyping and Prejudice against Older Persons. Cambridge: MIT Press.

Neugart, M., & Schömann, K. (2002). Why forecast and for whom? Some introductory remarks. In M. Neugart, & K. Schömann (Eds.), Forecasting Labour Markets in OECD Countries (pp. 1-25). Cheltenham: Edward Elgar.

Ng, T. W. H., & Feldman, D. C. (2008). The relationship of age to ten dimensions of job performance. *Journal of Applied Psychology, 93*, 392-423.

Noack, M., & Staudinger, U. M. (2007). Altersklima in Organisationen. Vorstellung eines Meßinstrumentes. Poster at the 5th Meeting of the I/O Psychology Group of the German Psychological Society, Trier (Germany).

OECD (2003). Beyond Rhetoric: Adult Learning Policies and Practices. Paris: OECD Publications.

OECD (2004). Lifelong Learning. Policy Brief. February 2004. Paris: OECD Publications.

OECD (2004b). Career Guidance. A Handbook for Policy Makers. Paris: OECD Publications.

OECD (2005). Promoting Adult Learning. Paris: OECD Publications.

OECD (2007). Qualifications Systems. Bridges to Lifelong Learning. Paris: OECD Publications.

Palincsar, A. S., & Brown, A. L. (1984). Reciprocal teaching of comprehension-fostering and comprehension-monitoring activities. *Cognition and Instruction,* 7, 117-175.

Paris, S. G., & Jacobs, J. E. (1984). The benefits of informed instruction for children's reading awareness and comprehension skills. *Child Development,* 55, 2083-2093.

Park, D. C. (2000). The basic mechanisms accounting for age-related decline in cognitive function. In D. C. Park, & N. Schwarz (Eds.*),* *Cognitive Aging.* A Primer (pp. 3-21). Philadelphia: Taylor & Francis.

Paulsson, K., Ivergård, T., & Hunt, B. (2005). Learning at work: competence development or competence-stress. *Applied Ergonomics,* 36, 135–144

Phillips, L. H., Kliegel, M., & Martin, M. (2006). Age and planning tasks: The influence of ecological validity. *International Journal of Aging and Human Development,* 62, 175-184.

Richter, F. (2005). Lernförderlichkeit der Arbeitssituation und Entwicklung beruflicher Handlungskompetenz. Hamburg: Kovac.

Salthouse, T. A. (1984). Effects of age and skill in typing. *Journal of Experimental Psychology: General,* 113, 345-371.

Schaie, K. W. (2005). Developmental Influences on Adult Intelligence: The Seattle Longitudinal Study. New York: Oxford University Press.

Schömann, K., & Siarov L. (2005). Sharing Costs and Responsibilities for Lifelong Learning. Paper prepared for the thematic review seminar of the mutual learning programme of the Commission of the European Communities, Brussels, 28. September 2005. http://www.mutual-learning-employment

Schömann, K., & Leschke, J. (2004). Lebenslanges Lernen und soziale Inklusion – Der Markt alleine wird's nicht richten. In R. Becker, & W. Lauterbach (Eds.), Bildung als Privileg? Theoretische Erklärungen und empirische Befunde zu den Ursachen der Bildungsungleichheiten (pp. 343-379). Wiesbaden: VS Verlag für Sozialwissenschaften.

Schulz, M., & Stamov Roßnagel, C. (in press). Informal workplace learning: An exploration of age differences in learning competence. *Learning and Instruction.*

Siegrist, J., & Marmot, M. (2004). Health inequalities and the psychosocial environment – two scientific challenges. *Social Sciences & Medicine,* 58, 1463-1473.

Simon, R. (1996). Too damn old. *Money,* 25, 118-126.

Stamov Roßnagel, C., Schulz, M., Picard, M., & Voelpel, S. (2009). Older workers' informal learning competency: Insights from a researcher-practitioner co-operation. Zeitschrift für Personalpsychologie, Special Issue: Demographic Change in Work Organizations, 8, 71-76.

Stine-Morrow, E.-A. L., Shake, M.-C., Miles, J.-R., & Noh, S.-R. (2006). Adult age differences in the effects of goals on self-regulated sentence processing. *Psychology and Aging,* 21(4), 790-803.

Streumer, J. (2004). Work Related Learning. Dordrecht: Kluwer.

Taris, T. W., Kompier, M. A. J., De Lange, A. H., Schaufeli, W. B., & Schreurs, P. J. G. (2003). Learning new behaviour patterns: a longitudinal test of Karasek's active learning hypothesis among Dutch teachers. *Work & Stress,* 17, 1-20.

Terman, L. M. (1916). The Measurement of Intelligence. Boston: Houghton.

Tornstam, L. (1992). The quo vadis of gerontology: on the scientific paradigm of gerontology. *Gerontologist,* 32, 318-326.

Tracey, J. B., & Tews, M. J. (2005). Construct validity of a general training climate scale. *Organizational Research Methods.* 8, 353-374.

Vaupel, J. W., & Loichinger, E. (2006). Redistributing work in aging Europe. *Science,* 312, 1911-1913.

Weinert, F. E. (1999). Concepts of Competence. München: Max Planck Institute for Psychological Research.

Weinstein, C. E., & Mayer, R. E. (1986). The teaching of learning strategies. In M. C. Wittrock (Ed.), *Handbook of Research on Teaching* (3rd ed., pp. 315-327). New York: MacMillan.

Wolf, O. T. (2003). HPA axis and memory. Best Practice & Research. *Clinical Endocrinology & Metabolism* 17, 287-299.

Wolf, O. T. (2007). The positive and the negative glucocorticoid effects on memory. In G. Fink (Ed.), *Encyclopedia of stress* (2nd revised ed., Vol. 1, pp. 166-171). Oxford: Academic Press.

Yerkes, R. M. (1921). Psychological examining in the United States Army. *Memoirs of the National Academy of Sciences,* 15, 1–890.

Zelinski, E. M., & Gilewski, M. J. (2004). A 10-item Rasch modeled memory self-efficacy scale. *Aging & Mental Health,* 8, 293-306.

INDEX

D

E

F

G